To someone who has made such a wonderful difference in my life

In case I never get around
to finding the perfect words
to say this in person,
I want to tell you now...

I admire you enormously.
I appreciate you immensely.
I think of you more than
 you'll ever know.

And you'll always hold
 a special place in my heart.

Other Books by Douglas Pagels
Published by
Blue Mountain Arts®

Chasing Away the Clouds

*Every Daughter Should Have a Book like This
to Remind Her How Wonderful She Is*

*Everyone Should Have a Book like This
to Get Through the Gray Days*

For You, Just Because You're Very Special to Me

I Want You to Read This Today...

A Keepsake for My Children

100 Things to Always Remember...

Required Reading for All Teenagers

30 Beautiful Things That Are True About You

To the One Person I Consider to Be My Soul Mate

Copyright © 2006 by Blue Mountain Arts, Inc.

All writings are by Douglas Pagels except as noted.

Library of Congress Control Number: 2006902085
ISBN-13: 978-1-59842-168-2
ISBN-10: 1-59842-168-9

Certain trademarks are used under license.
BLUE MOUNTAIN PRESS is registered in U.S. Patent and Trademark Office.

Acknowledgments appear on page 4.

Manufactured in the United States of America.
First Printing: 2006

 This book is printed on recycled paper.

This book is printed on fine quality, laid embossed, 80 lb. paper. This paper has been specially produced to be acid free (neutral pH) and contains no groundwood or unbleached pulp. It conforms with the requirements of the American National Standards Institute, Inc., so as to ensure that this book will last and be enjoyed by future generations.

Blue Mountain Arts, Inc.
P.O. Box 4549, Boulder, Colorado 80306

Everyone
should have
a book
like this
to share
with a special

FRIEND

Douglas Pagels

Blue Mountain Press ®

Boulder, Colorado

ACKNOWLEDGMENTS

We gratefully acknowledge the permission granted by the following authors, publishers, and authors' representatives to reprint poems or excerpts from their publications.

Warner Brothers Music Corp. and New Hidden Valley Music for "Keep smiling, keep shining..." from "That's What Friends Are For" by Carole Bayer Sager and Burt Bacharach. Copyright © 1982, 1985 by Warner Brothers Music Corp., New Hidden Valley Music, Warner-Tamerlane Publishing Corp., and Carole Bayer Sager Music. All rights on behalf of New Hidden Valley Music administered by Warner Brothers Music Corp. All rights on behalf of Carole Bayer Sager Music administered by Warner-Tamerlane Publishing Corp. All rights reserved.

Riverhead Books, an imprint of Penguin Group (USA), Inc., and Ed Victor, Ltd., for "I can't remember his quote exactly..." by Bono from BONO: IN CONVERSATIONS WITH MICHKA ASSAYAS by Michka Assayas. Copyright © 2005 by Michka Assayas. All rights reserved.

John Wiley and Sons, Inc., for "My friends are my family" by Oprah Winfrey from OPRAH WINFREY SPEAKS by Janet Lowe. Copyright © 1998 by Janet Lowe. All rights reserved.

Doubleday, a division of Random House, Inc., for "'Ahhhh, it's my buddy...'" by Morrie Schwartz from TUESDAYS WITH MORRIE by Mitch Albom. Copyright © 1997 by Mitch Albom. All rights reserved.

HarperCollins Publishers for "My friends are a blessing..." from LADIES FIRST by Queen Latifah. Copyright © 1999 by Queen Latifah, Inc. All rights reserved.

Alfred A. Knopf, a division of Random House, Inc., for "Those special friends..." from NOW by Lauren Bacall. Copyright © 1994 by Caprigo, Inc. All rights reserved.

Regnery Publishing, Inc., Washington, DC, for "I'd like to be the sort of friend..." from COLLECTED VERSE OF EDGAR A. GUEST by Edgar A. Guest. Copyright © 1934 by Henry Regnery Publishing, Inc. All rights reserved.

Villard Books, a division of Random House, Inc., for "What makes someone feel like a true friend?" from SECRETS OF A SPARROW by Diana Ross. Copyright © 1993 by Diana Ross. All rights reserved.

Hachette Book Group USA for "I never felt so alone in my life..." from 700 SUNDAYS by Billy Crystal. Copyright © 2005 by Billy Crystal. Reprinted by permission of Hachette Book Group USA. All rights reserved.

Random House, Inc., for "We reached that point in closeness..." from NEVER HAVE YOUR DOG STUFFED by Alan Alda. Copyright © 2005 by Mayflower Productions, Inc. All rights reserved.

Houghton Mifflin Company for "Friendship is like tennis..." from VENUS AND SERENA: SERVING FROM THE HIP by Venus Williams and Serena Williams. Copyright © 2005 by Venus Williams and Serena Williams. Reprinted by permission. All rights reserved.

Stephen Schwartz for "So let me say before we part..." from "For Good" from the Broadway Musical *Wicked*. Music and lyrics by Stephen Schwartz. Copyright © 2003 by Stephen Schwartz. All rights reserved.

A careful effort has been made to trace the ownership of selections used in this anthology in order to obtain permission to reprint copyrighted material and give proper credit to the copyright owners. If any error or omission has occurred, it is completely inadvertent, and we would like to make corrections in future editions provided that written notification is made to the publisher:

BLUE MOUNTAIN ARTS, INC., P.O. Box 4549, Boulder, Colorado 80306.

Contents

Remember What Carole and Burt Said...

Keep smiling, keep shining,
Knowing you can always
count on me...

For good times
and bad times
I'll be on your side
forevermore

That's what friends are for.

— Carole Bayer Sager
and Burt Bacharach

A Friend Is...

A friend is one of the nicest things you can have, and one of the best things you can be. A friend is a living treasure, and if you have one, you have one of the most valuable gifts in life...

A friend is the one who will always be beside you, through all the laughter and through each and every tear.
A friend is the one thing you can always rely on; the someone you can always open up to; the one wonderful person who always believes in you in a way that no one else seems to.

A friend is a sanctuary.
A friend is a smile.

A friend is a hand that is always
holding yours, no matter where you
are, no matter how close or far apart
you may be...

A friend is someone who is always
there and will always — always — care.
A friend is a feeling of forever in
    the heart.

A friend is the one door that is
    always open.
A friend is the one to whom you
    can give your key.
A friend is one of the nicest things
    you can have, and one of the
        best things you can be.

Remember What Bono Said...

I can't remember his quote exactly, but there is a writing by Jean Cocteau where he says friendship is higher than love. Sometimes, it's less glamorous... but it's deeper and kind of wiser, I think.

— Bono

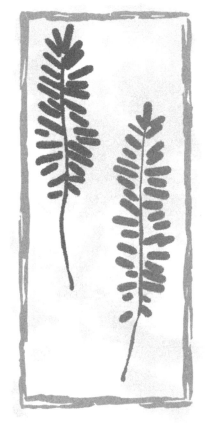

What Friends
Are Best At

Friends are best at…
every single thing
that brings joy to the heart.

Friends are best at…
being generous, giving, and forgiving.
Lifting spirits. Understanding.
Being there through thick and thin.
Nourishing your inner life.
Making your outer life smile and
      grin and laugh out loud.

Friends are best at…
contributing immensely to your happiness.
Restoring and renewing.
Propping up your self-esteem.
Being the strongest support system ever.
Filling any emptiness inside.
Making your heart overflow with gratitude.

Friends are best at…
making life's journey so much sweeter.
Feeling the same way about so many things.
Communicating on the same wavelength.

Remember What
Oprah Said...

My friends are
my family.

— Oprah Winfrey

Friends are best at...
being so close. Feeling like family.
Deep devotion, passing every test of time.
Checking in regularly to get all the latest news.
Always being able to read between the lines.
Never feeling any distance between them...
or any days apart, because their lives
are so tenderly connected to one another.

Friends are beautiful souls who
have something that will last...

and bless their lives
forever.

It seems like I'm always searching
for a way to tell you
how wonderful I think you are.

And I thought that maybe
this book could help me
convey a few thoughts
    that I would love to share with you...

You're my definition of a special person.

I think you're fantastic. And
exceptional and unique and endearing.
To me, you're someone
who is very necessary to my well-being.
In so many ways, you fill my life
with happiness and the sweet feelings
of being so grateful and appreciative
    that you're here.

I could go on and on...
    but you get the picture.

I think you're a masterpiece.

If we haven't seen each other in a while, there's this magical, amazing thing that happens with us. We pick up... right where we left off. It's almost like no time passed at all.

The clock may as well have stopped the moment we parted and started up again the next time we met. The same closeness, the same smiling eyes, the same... everything is there. It is an enriching and reaffirming experience whenever that happens, and it doesn't happen unless the bond was a wonderful one to begin with.

That's just how it is... when you have a very special friend.

And that's exactly how it is... with us.

Remember What
This Says...

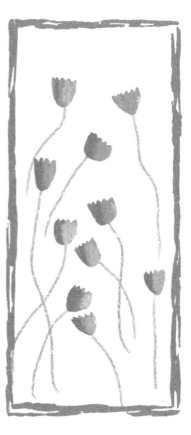

You don't need a certain
number of friends, only
a number of friends you
can be certain of.

— Anonymous

The wealthiest people in the world are
the people whose friendships are going
    to last a lifetime...
no matter what, no matter where,
whether they're close together or
separated by thousands of miles. Those
are the kind of friendships that give
more joy and hope and help to your
days than anything else could ever do,
and they make your days as rich as
anything could ever be.

Friends bring sunlight into your life. They warm your life with their presence, whether they are far away or close by your side. A friend is a gift that brings happiness, and a treasure that money can't buy.

Remember What
Mitch and Morrie Said...

"Ahhhh, it's my buddy," he would say when he saw me.... And it didn't stop with the greeting. When Morrie was with you, he was really with you. He looked you straight in the eye, and he listened as if you were the only person in the world.

— Mitch Albom and
Morrie Schwartz

This is what friendship looks like...

It looks like two people who see all the best qualities in one another. Who give each other a ton of love, who cut each other a lot of slack, and who provide more open, honest, and real communication than any "outsider" could ever begin to do. It looks like two people who are exceedingly comfortable with one another, serenely confident about their bond, and supremely lucky to have someone so great to be able to count on. It looks like two people whose lives are so much more wonderful together than they could ever be apart.

For keeping my spirits up.
For never letting me down.
For being here for me.
For knowing I'm there for you.

For bringing so many smiles my way.
For being sensitive to my needs.
For knowing just what to say.
For listening better than anyone else.

For bringing me laughter.
For bringing me light.
For understanding so much about me.
For trusting me with so much about you.

For being the best.
For being so beautiful.

    I don't know what I'd do
        ...without you.

This is what friendship feels like...

It feels like one of the most beautiful things imaginable. It feels strong and happy and safe. It feels like a privilege. And even though it never gets taken for granted, it feels like everything is simply understood. It feels like the sharing of a special moment in time. It feels like being in the middle of a lifelong adventure that just gets more and more meaningful as the miles go by and the years continue on. It feels like a continuous celebration of all the joy it brings.

Remember What
Queen Latifah Said…

My friends are a blessing.... When I am around my friends I feel *good*. I feel *secure*. Our friendship is based on something that is completely unspoken: trust. And that trust, combined with years of experiences together, has forged a bond of understanding and unconditional love.

— Queen Latifah

The Beautiful Difference

I guess you could say that there are times when it seems like I'm two different people. I'm a certain way when I'm with everyone else... and another way (more real and relaxed, more honest and open)... with you.

When I'm with other people, I usually stay on the safe side. I know how vulnerable I can be and I don't leave myself open to things that trouble me. Sometimes I realize what a burden I've been carrying around; it can be hard work dealing with all the things I put in place to protect my feelings.

But then... I get together with you...
and the whole world is dramatically
different. It's refreshing, peaceful, and
perfectly at ease. It's wonderful... being
in the company of someone like you.

There are probably times when you can
hear my sigh of relief for miles around!

It's like... "Everything is okay now.
 I'm with my good friend.
  I get to let my guard down."

Remember What
Samuel and Emily Said…

Friendship is a
sheltering tree.

— Samuel Taylor Coleridge

I felt it shelter
to speak to you.

— Emily Dickinson

This is what friendship sounds like…

Even from a distance, you can hear their laughter. From up close, you can hear their trust. It comes out in the spontaneity, the openness, the complete lack of fussing about whether it's "okay to say this or not?" Of course it's okay. If it comes from the heart and the soul… it doesn't have to go through a translator or a filter before it is spoken to a friend. That's the beauty of it all. Friendship speaks the truth, and when you hear it, it fills you with a light that warms you with kindness and reassurance.

For You

I don't know exactly what it is... but there is something very special about you.

It might be all the things I see on the surface: things that everyone notices and admires about you. Qualities and capabilities. Your wonderful smile, obviously connected to a warm and loving heart. It might be all the things that set you apart from everyone else.

Maybe it's the way you never hesitate to go a million miles out of your way to help out. The way your todays help set the stage for so many beautiful tomorrows. Or maybe it's the way your words always come straight from the heart.

If I could ever figure out all the magic
that makes you so special, I'd probably
find out that it's a combination of all these
attributes — blended together with some
of the best things this world has to offer:
Making memories. Sharing feelings. Precious
togetherness. And simply being someone
whose light shines brighter than any star.

You really are amazing.

And I feel very lucky
to have been given the gift
of knowing how special
    you are.

If someone were to ask me...

...the secrets of happiness and
gratitude and serenity, I know
exactly what I'd do.

I'd tell them to make sure
that they have a person
in their lives
who's as precious,
as special,
and as wonderful...

as you.

Remember What
Lauren Said...

Those special friends whom
I am closest to... interest
me: how they think, what
they feel, how they deal
with life — its gifts and its
denials. They add to and
complete the circle of my
life and enrich me. They
are what I hang on to.

— Lauren Bacall

Friendship Is like a Promise You Keep in Your Heart

I have been blessed by our friendship for such a long time. I hope you know — deep inside — what a joy it is to my life and what a privilege I consider it to be.

Our friendship means the world to me, and I want you to know that I'll never take it for granted. It is a tremendously sweet responsibility to be your friend. It means acting directly from the heart and being there for you... from the littlest thing to the largest issues we'll ever be faced with.

Because we're as close as we are, there are lots of opportunities for us to be there for one another. The moments spent in the circle of our friendship are some of the finest times I'll ever have.

I feel so honored to have you confide in me about your life… about your family, your work, your cares and concerns, your hopes and dreams… about everything.

And I am equally honored to be able to share feelings about all the different aspects of my life with you. Whether the news is good or bad, whether my words are those of celebration or sadness, it is reassuring to be able to turn to you. When the two of us speak, the truth can always be shared… because the trust is always there.

Our friendship feels like a promise that we keep in our hearts… a promise that grows stronger and more rewarding with the passing years. And it's a promise that blesses my days and brightens up my entire life.

Remember What
Edgar Said…

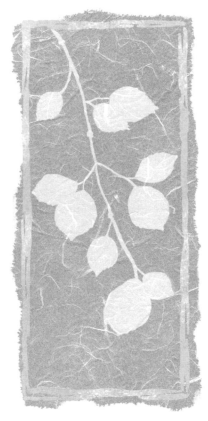

I'd like to be the sort of friend
  that you have been to me;
I'd like to be the help that
  you've been always glad to be;
I'd like to mean as much to you
  each minute of the day
As you have meant, old friend
  of mine, to me along the way.

— Edgar A. Guest

Friendship

Friendship begins with meeting someone along the path of life. Someone you get to know, and gradually get to know even better. You discover what a joy it is to spend your moments with this person.

It's nice the way the good feelings of friendship remain. The happiness lasts, and the memories you make start to turn into some of your favorite treasures. Friendship is two paths converging on the way to the same beautiful view.

Friendship is walking the way together.

This is for you, for being someone whose soul is so inspiring. This is a "thank you" for having a heart that's so big and a mind that is so open. And a spirit that I really love.

It's a message of gratitude for an incredibly special person. You inspire me with your wonderfulness. You're the first person I think of whenever I have something to share, and you're the last person in the universe I would hurt or ever be unkind to. You are a treasure to my life, and I value you so much. You have an amazing knack for reassuring me.

You invite me to go along to the places your journeys take you... when you dream, when you wonder, and when you reminisce...

And you let me know that you're a willing traveling companion, happy to join me in all my journeys, too.

I love that about you. I cherish the fact that you understand me so well and that I know you just about as well as I could ever know anyone.

I am blessed by the thousands of smiles we have shared, by the laughter that lingers in my heart, and by our concerns that have found a place of comfort in the sanctuary of our caring. I truly don't know what I'd do... without the goodness you give my life.

Friendship is opening up to one another.
Sharing thoughts and feelings in a way
that never felt this comfortable before.

It is a complete trust, sweetened with a
lot more understanding and communication
than many people will ever know.

Friendship is two hearts that are able
to say things no outsiders ever could.

Remember What
Diana Said...

What makes someone feel
like a true friend? I think it
is the ease in communication,
the feeling of not being
afraid to trust someone with
your heart and your most
private feelings.

— Diana Ross

The luckiest people in the world
are those who have a wonderful friend
    to share life with...
a friend who cares and who shares the gifts
of smiles and closeness and companionship.
Someone with whom you have so much in
common. Somebody who's a precious part
of the best memories you'll ever make. A
special friend. A true friend.

One to confide in, one who never lets you down, and one who always understands. A friend who is simply amazing… whose heart is so big, soul is so beautiful, and because everything about this friend inspires everything that is good about you.

Remember What
Billy Said...

I never felt so alone in my life, and then I looked up, and three of my friends... walked in.

They had made their way to the Bronx to be with me... I couldn't believe that they came. We all hugged, and when Mom saw them, she shook her head in wonder, and said, "Friends, such good friends."

— Billy Crystal

Friends do things for one another. They understand. They reach out. They hold your hand. They bring you smiles, when a smile is exactly what you need. They listen, and they hear what is said in the spaces between the words. They care. And they let you know you're in their prayers.

A friend can guide you, inspire you, comfort you, and light up your life.

You are very important to me.
   And I'll try to tell you why...

You and I share so much of what is good about life.
Things like... so many experiences
   that only you and I have known.
And so many personal feelings and emotions
   that we have shown only to each other.

With us, the ordinary times turn into great times
and simple conversations turn into honest,
   trusting talks.

With us, so much is understood. So much is
everything it should be... and more.

Laughter is natural and easy. Sentiment is shared.
Hard times are softened. And the more often I think
     about you, the more wonderful I realize you are.
Whether I'm alone, or we're talking on the phone,
     or we're taking a long walk,
I know how much we both care... and I cherish
     knowing that it will always be that way.

In the dance of life, friends are. the people who encourage you to be your best, who like you for who you are, who remind you what steps to take when you've forgotten the way, and who help you rest assured that your secrets are safe and your hopes are in good hands.

They help to balance things out, they keep you on your toes, they make you smile even when you're stumbling through life, and the stories, support, and laughter they bring to the years feel more like music to your ears than just about anything.

Remember What
Alan Said…

We reached that point in closeness where you become aware of the other person's imperfections as they become aware of yours, and you either stick it out with them or walk the other way. We stuck it out. And… looked for compromises. But mostly we made one another laugh. And it was the laughing, even more than the compromises, that led to trust. This was good, because trust is where the gold is.

— Alan Alda

In the Good Days

Friends... are the kindred
spirits who never laugh at
you, but who have a
knack of laughing *with*
you a million times better
than anyone else.

In the Gray Days

Friends... are the precious
people who dry the tears
that no one else can
even see.

In the Golden Days

Friends... are the special people you're drawn to, sometimes for reasons you're not even sure of... except for a feeling deep inside that says yes, this is someone to be trusted, this is something that is very rare, and this is somebody you're going to be able to share one of life's best treasures with.

Some friends seem so meant to be. And you were exactly like that for me. We've always just "clicked" and been so connected. And I know we'll stay that way till we're old and gray and waltzing off into the sunset on some distant shore.

Thank you, my friend, for being such a beautiful part of the song in my heart and the story of my life.

Remember What Venus and Serena Said…

Friendship is like tennis — it's all about the back and forth.

— Venus and Serena Williams

There's nothing I'd like better than to be able to return the favor… of your warmth and wonder and generosity. You bring happiness to me when the world seems to be wearing a frown. When things don't quite go as planned and my world seems upside down, my thoughts of you help to set things right again.

You are so important to me! You make me think, you make me laugh, you make me feel alive. You put things in perspective for me. You provide support and encouragement, you lessen my worries, and you increase my joys.

One of the hopes I'll have my whole life through… is to be able to do those things for you, too.

Lessons I've Learned
from a Wonderful Friendship

*≈ With others, you have minutes in the day.
With friends, you share moments in time. ≈*

There's a big difference between spending time with
most people in life… and spending time with a friend.
Many people barely connect; the rush-about world
doesn't allow for much of an opportunity to move
beyond the surface sort of interaction or the simple
sharing of minutes in the day.

But when I'm with you, my friend, everything is
different. The world slows down. The sun comes out.
Things that haven't seen the light of day in a while
suddenly become clearer and brighter. Things are so
much nicer. Words come easily, freely, truthfully.

Because our friendship is so important to me, our
times together take on so much significance. When
I'm with you, a little walk can turn into an adventure,
a brief conversation can capture absolutely everything
that's on our minds, and our minutes can turn into
moments… that mean the world to me.

*≈ Between friends, trust is the treasure...
and staying close, whether you're together
or apart, is the key. ≈*

There is a foundation we've built, and it's solid and certain and more reassuring than my words can begin to say. There's the sweet feeling that we can spend the day doing everything or nothing at all... and that regardless of what we choose to do, we will have a better time than anyone could ever imagine.

Together, without even trying to, you and I always manage to make the most of the moments we're given. And in so doing, I think we add a tremendous amount of meaning and comfort and wonder to the moments we have... and to the lives we are living.

*≈ Friendship is such a gift. It makes beautiful
memories to sweeten the past, and it reminds us
almost every day how much there is to appreciate
in the present. ≈*

We have a bond that
    will always be there for us.

No matter where we go
    or how much time passes,
    you and I will always,
    in a very special way,
    remain together in spirit.
And that knowledge is
    cherished by me as the one
    thing that must never change.

In a world of constant transition,
    I pray that what we feel
        toward one another
            will *always* stay the same.

Remember What
Stephen Said…

So let me say
   before we part
So much of me
Is made of what I learned
   from you
You'll be with me
Like a handprint
   on my heart

And now whatever way
   our stories end
I know you have
   re-written mine
By being my friend

— Stephen Schwartz

I think that... in the same way
that the brightest stars are always
shining in the sky... the most
wonderful people in our lives take
up a special place in our hearts
and remain with us forever.

I am so thankful that the joys
you inspire, the understanding
you are graced with, and the
closeness that has blessed us in
so many ways... all came into
my world.

There are no words to tell you
what a difference you have made.

Every smile, every kindness,
every day we have had the privilege
of sharing together... so many
things will live on in my life
and brighten so many moments
in my heart's memory. I will
always think of them as such
beautiful gifts.

And I'll never forget
who gave them... to me.

And Remember
What I Said...

Forever and ever
I will have a smile
inside of me
that belongs to you.

— Douglas Pagels